BOL

Collection fondé

THE FORD POWDER MILL, MORRISTOWN, N. J., 1776. See page 189

THE MAJOR JOSEPH LINDSLEY HOUSE NEAR FORD'S POWDER MILL,
MORRISTOWN, N. J.

BROWN AND BEAR OR THE OTHERWISE GROWTH TREE TO THE SOUTHEASTWARD OF THE NEW JERSEY

Jacob Johnson

C Russells

THE OLD TUTTLE HOUSE ON THE
JOCKEY HOLLOW ROAD.

"MAD" ANTHONY WAYN

Reca⁰ Eight pounds with the Interest for one year
being the Money Herr Timothy Johnes Jr at the time
I gave the Bond for one hundred & twenty Pounds in
Company with Daniel Hafey and Indorst it on the Bond
without Pay for one years Interest as witness my
hand this twenty Second Day of March 1788
    Jacob Arnold

MONUMENT TO REVOLUTIONARY SOLDIERS IN THE PRESBYTERIAN
BURIAL GROUNDS, MORRISTOWN, N. J.

LEDDELL'S MILLS.

 See page 354

THE ARNOLD TAVERN, MORRISTOWN. N. J.

Photo. by J. Elbert Eckert.

SITE OF THE "GRAND PARADE." LOOKING NORTHEASTERLY. SUGAR LOAF ON THE LEFT. THE JOCKEY HOLLOW ROAD TO THE RIGHT.

See page 305

THE ROAD OVER WHICH WASHINGTON'S ARMY CAME TO LOWANTICA
IN 1777   See page 212

LAKE FED BY SPRINGS FROM WHICH WASHINGTON'S ARMY PROCURED WATER IN 1777.
See page 216

SITE OF THE LARZELEAR TAVERN ON THE BASKING RIDGE ROAD.

THE CLUMP OF LOCUSTS WHERE ONE HUNDRED REVOLUTIONARY SOLDIERS ARE BURIED.

See page 289

CORNER OF THE BASKING RIDGE AND NEW VERNON ROADS THREE MILES SOUTH OF THE MORRISTOWN GREEN.

SPEAR FOUND IN THE CELLAR OF THE ARNOLD TAVERN, MORRISTOWN, N. J.

Andrew M. Sherman.

SCENE OF GENERAL WAYNE'S ENCOUNTER WITH THE
PENNSYLVANIA MUTINEERS.   See page 375

HORSEHEAD PENNY—SHOWING EACH SIDE.   See page 404

INTERSECTION OF THE JOCKEY HOLLOW AND MENDHAM ROADS.

Photo. by J. Elbert Egbert.

PILE OF HUT CHIMNEY-STONES ON THE NEW JERSEY BRIGADE CAMP GROUND OF 1779-80, FOOT OF BLACHLY HILL.

See page 299

FLAGLER'S OR DURLING'S MILL, MORRISTOWN, N. J.

See page 24

FIRST WORDS OF INDIAN DEED.

See page 18

LAFAYETTE.

PHILIP SCHUYLER.

GENERAL MARION.

ROBERT MORRIS.

THADDEUS KOSCIUSKO.

GENERAL BENEDICT ARNOLD.

COL. JACOB ARNOLD'S WATCH,
CHAIN AND SEAL.

See page 183

THE WICKE HOUSE.

See page 381

LOOKING UP SPRING VALLEY FROM THE LOWANTICA CAMP GROUND.

See page 212

THE STARK MONUMENT.

See page 282

Photo. by J. Elbert Egbert.

PILE OF HUT CHIMNEY-STONES ON THE CONNECTICUT BRIGADE CAMP
GROUND OF 1779-80.   See page 235

SITE OF STARK'S BRIGADE CAMP GROUND IN 1779-80 SHOWING THE
STARK MONUMENT.   See page 281

SITE OF THE FIRST MARYLAND BRIGADE CAMP GROUND IN 1779-80.
See page 272

LEDDELL'S POND.

THE DR. LEDDELL HOUSE. See page 352

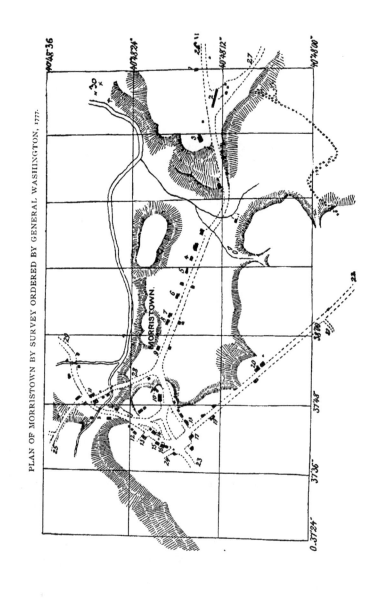

PLAN OF MORRISTOWN BY SURVEY ORDERED BY GENERAL WASHINGTON, 1777.

1—Squire Benjamin Lindsley; about where summer house is located in front of the late residence of Dr. J. Smith Dodge.

2—Life guard hut.

3—Washington's Headquarters.

4—Dr. Jabez Campfield; house now owned by James Clark, on right of Olyphant lane.

5—Frederick King; corner Olyphant lane and Morris street, formerly known as the Duncan house, now owned by Joseph York.

6—Occupied by Major Mahlon Ford at the beginning of the last century; not standing now.

7—Old Dickerson house; not known by whom occupied during the Revolutionary War; about in centre of present depot plaza.

8—Colonel Joseph Lewis; now owned by the Lackawanna Railroad Company.

9—Rev. Timothy Johnes; present site of Memorial Hospital.

10—Presbyterian Church.

11—Norris's Tavern, eastern corner Spring and Water street, where yellow house now stands.

12—Baptist Church; about where the old Baptist Church stood; present McAlpin building.

13—Colonel Henry Remsen.

14—Courthouse and Jail; opposite United States Hotel, about centre of street, West Park place.

15—Curtis's store.

16—Arnold Tavern; present site of "The Arnold," now "Hoffman" Building.

17—Continental stores; present site of National Bank.

18—Ex-Sheriff Carmichael; present site of Western Union Telegraph Office.

19—Lieutenant-Colonel William De Hart; now owned by Dr. Henry N. Dodge.

20—Squire Samuel Tuthill.

21—Present James street.

22—South street.

23—Basking Ridge road; present Market street and Mt. Kemble avenue.

24—Jockey Hollow road, now Western avenue.

25—Mendham road, now Early street.

26—Whippany road, now Morris street and avenue.

27—Bottle Hill road, now Washington avenue.

28—Present Spring street.

29—Present Water street.

See page 117.

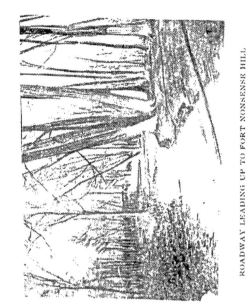

ROADWAY LEADING UP TO FORT NONSENSE HILL, MORRISTOWN, N. J.

RUINS OF STONE BAKE-OVEN ON THE JOCKEY HOLLOW ROAD.

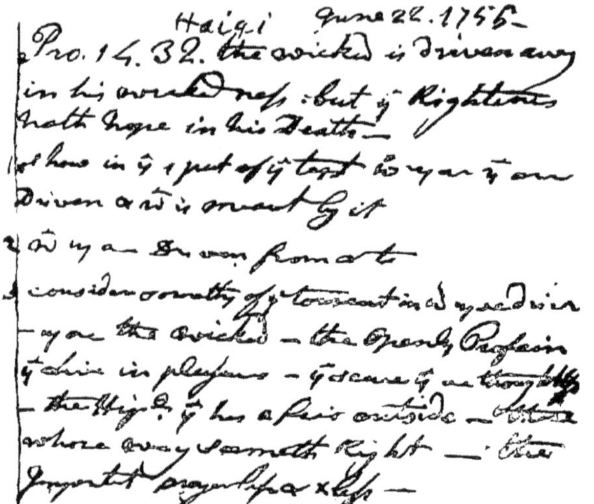

ONE PAGE OF DR. TIMOTHY JOHNE'S SERMON NOTES.

OLD FASHIONED FIREPLACE AND HOUSEHOLD IMPLEMENTS.

SITE OF QUARTERMASTER-GENERAL GREENE'S OFFICE IN 1777. See page 221

WASHINGTON HEADQUARTERS, MORRISTOWN, N. J.

RUINS OF STONE BAKE-OVEN USED BY ONE OF THE MARYLAND
BRIGADES IN 1779-80. See page 293

BLACK OAK TREE WHERE CAPTAIN BETTIN IS BURIED. See page 374

IN MEMORY OF
CAPTAIN ADAM BETTIN
SHOT IN THE MUTINY
JAN 1 1781
ERECTED BY THE
MORRISTOWN CHAPTER
D. A. R.

THE BETTIN MONUMENT SHOWING THE INSCRIPTION. See page 374

JOS. LEWIS.

This Picture was made from a Miniature Portrait in Oil
loaned by Mrs. E. Anna Dickerson, of Bloomfield, N. J.,
who is a Granddaughter of General Joseph Lewis and a
Great-granddaughter of Parson Johnes.

SITE OF THE NEW YORK BRIGADE CAMP GROUND IN 1779-80. "OLD TUTTLE HOUSE" ON THE RIGHT.
THE JOCKEY HOLLOW ROAD IN THE LEFT BACKGROUND LEADING TOWARD MORRISTOWN.

SITE OF THE CAPT. AUGUSTINE BAYLEY HOUSE ON THE JOCKEY HOLLOW ROAD.
THE AMZI PIERSON HOUSE ON THE LEFT.

Photo. by J. Elbert Egbert

See page 371

DICKERSON'S TAVERN, "UNDER THE HILL."

See page 163

SITE OF THE PRIMITIVE BAPTIST CHURCH OF MORRISTOWN, N. J.

See page 80

BOULDER ERECTED BY THE D. A. R. ON THE
MORRISTOWN GREEN.

See page 71

THE OLD COUNTY COURTHOUSE ON THE MORRISTOWN GREEN.

See page 68

LOCALITY FIRST SETTLED IN MORRISTOWN, N.

WHIPPANY, N. J., BURIAL GROUNDS.

See page 32

About the year 1710 2 pure families moved from Newark & Elizabeth Town — & settled on the — west side of Pequick River in that — which is now Morris county. Not long after the settlers erected an house on the publick worship of God on the the bank of Whippanung River (about three miles west of Pequick River;) about one hundred rods below the Forge which is & has long been known by the name of the old Iron works. There was a ch[urch] gathered & in the year 17— M.r Nathanael Hubbol was ordained a settled there by the Presbytery of New York. about this time this place obtained the name of Hanover & become a Township, and the place was most commonly known by the Indian name Whippanung.

Jacob Green   Jacob Green Minister

EXTRACT FROM "PARSON GREEN'S" PARISH BOOK.

See page 5

SITE OF PETER KEMBLE'S HOUSE.

See page 229

THE KEMBLE BURIAL GROUND.

See page 231

MONUMENT OF COL. JACOB FORD, JR.,
MORRISTOWN, N. J

See page 205

SUN-DIAL MONUMENT. ERECTED
BY THE D. A. R. TO MARK THE
SITE OF THE DELL WHERE WASH-
INGTON PARTOOK OF THE LORD'S
SUPPER.

See page 237

MONUMENT OF COL. JACOB FORD, SR., MORRISTOWN, N. J.

See page 211

THE PRESBYTERIAN CHURCH, MORRISTOWN, N. J.,
DURING THE REVOLUTION.

Courtesy of Philip H. Hoffman

See page 48

PRESBYTERIAN CHURCH

PRESBYTERIAN CHURCH OF MORRISTOWN,
N. J., IN 1705.

Courtesy of Harris A. Freeman See page 432

THE CONTINENTAL STORE HOUSE (MORRISTOWN, N. J.) OF THE
REVOLUTIONARY PERIOD, AFTERWARD O'HARA'S TAVERN.

Courtesy of Philip H. Hoffman

See page 362

THE DEACON SAYRE PLACE AT BOTTLE HILL, N. J.

See page 378

LOOKING (NORTHEASTWARD) UP THE JOCKEY HOLLOW ROAD TOWARD
MORRISTOWN FROM THE MENDHAM ROAD. HAND'S BRIG-
ADE CAMP GROUND IN 1779-80 ON THE RIGHT.
Photo by J. Elbert Egbert

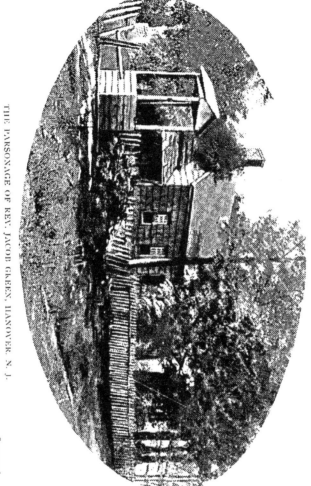

THE PARSONAGE OF REV. JACOB GREEN, HANOVER, N. J.

See page 6

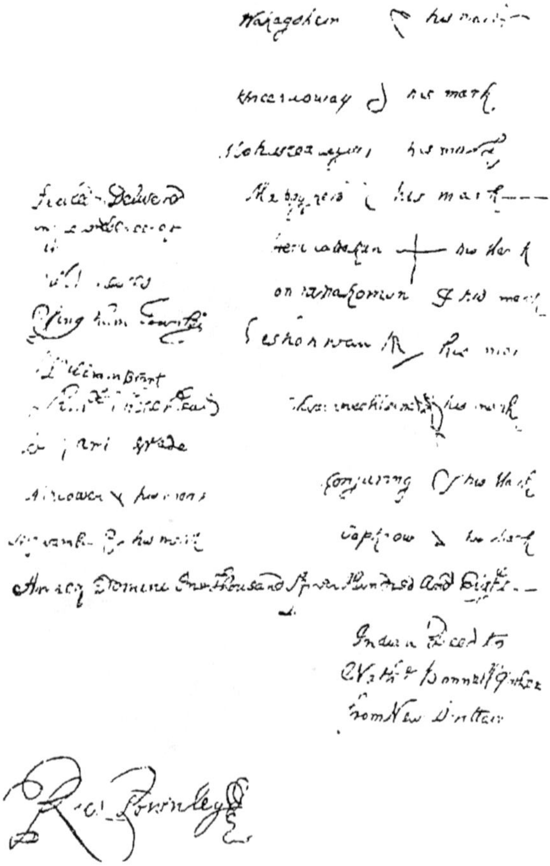

FAC-SIMILE SIGNATURES ON OLD INDIAN DEED.

See page 18

LOOKING (SOUTHEASTWARD) DOWN THE VALLEY OCCUPIED BY THE NEW JERSEY BRIGADE IN 1779-80.
BLACHLY HILL ON THE RIGHT. FORT HILL ON THE LEFT.

SITE OF THE PENNSYLVANIA BRIGADE CAMP GROUND IN 1779-80 LOOKING EASTWARD. KEMBLE
MOUNTAIN ON THE RIGHT. SUGAR LOAF ON THE LEFT. THE
"GROFF HOUSE" IN THE BACKGROUND.

Photo. by J. Elbert Egbert

See page 288

THE DR. JABEZ CAMPFIELD HOUSE. MORRISTOWN, N. J.
See page 363

SITE OF "THE HAMMOCK," MORRISTOWN, N. J.
See page 122

MONUMENT OF PETER CONDICT,
MORRISTOWN, N. J.

THE COL. HATHAWAY HOUSE, MORRISTOWN, N. J. See page 192

STONE MARKING THE CORNERSTONE OF THE FIRST PRESBYTERIAN
CHURCH IN MORRISTOWN.

See page 48

THE GENERAL DOUGHTY HOUSE, MORRISTOWN, N. J.

HOUSEHOLD IMPLEMENTS OF COLONIAL DAYS.

THE OLD BAPTIST CHURCH ON THE "MORRISTOWN GREEN."

See page 92

ROADWAY LEADING UP THE FORT NONSENSE HILL, MORRISTOWN, N. J.

SECTION (SOUTHEASTERLY) OF EARTHWORKS ON FORT NONSENSE
HILL, MORRISTOWN, N. J.

See page 269

THE OLD FAIRCHILD CONTINENTAL DRUM CORPS, MORRISTOWN N. J., ORGANIZED IN 1870. FROM LEFT TO RIGHT THE NAMES ARE: W MELL FAIRCHILD (DECEASED), HENRY H. FAIRCHILD (DECEASED), EX SHERIFF W. W. FAIRCHILD (DECEASED), CLIFFORD A. FAIRCHILD, FRANK H. FAIRCHILD.

RESIDENCE OF GUSTAV A. KISSELL, MORRISTOWN, N. J.

See page 405

SITE OF THE SILVER MINE ON THE OLD JUDGE SYMMES
PLACE, MORRISTOWN, N. J.

See page 406

THE SILAS CONDICT HOUSE, MORRISTOWN, N. J.   SHERMAN HILL IN
THE DISTANCE.

See page 223

MONUMENT ON FORT NONSENSE HILL ERECTED BY THE
WASHINGTON ASSOCIATION OF NEW JERSEY IN 1888.

Summits of Hills

A. Kemble's Mountain Alarm Station
F. Fort Hill
P. Picatinny
S. Sugar Loaf
T. Tea Hill

Houses in 1780

K. Kemble
W. Wick.
1. Guerin
2. Ferrer
3. Bayles
4. Coble, Robert ?
5. Coble, Jonas Jr.
6. Primrose

Relative Positions of the Ten Brigades.

BY PERMISSION OF EMORY McCLINTOCK, LL.D.

See page 301

THE JOSHUA GUERIN HOUSE ON THE JOCKEY HOLLOW ROAD.

ROAD LEADING TOWARD MENDHAM FROM HOYT'S CORNER.

RUINS OF A STONE BAKE-OVEN ON THE CONNECTICUT BRIGADE CAMP GROUND OF 1779-80.

Photo. by I. Elbert Egbert

See page 296

SECTION OF THE FORT HILL OF THE REVOLUTIONARY PERIOD
LOOKING TOWARD THE WICK HOUSE. THE CONNECTICUT
BRIGADE CAMP GROUND IS JUST TO THE RIGHT.

Photo by J. Elbert Egbert

Decemʳ. 14. 88.

Heb. 4. 9. ÿ remain ÿfore a rest to ÿ Peo.

1 say some. thing of ÿ rest ⟩
2 to whom 3 how it remaineth
— M. nat. as tis. Sea. — Gor. only G. Rest
1 a Sab. rest — institu. before ÿ fall
— & continu. ever since
2 a spi. Sab. — we ÿ ha. beli. do enter
in. rest 3. — do enter in. union w x
— in. commu w G thro x — & in ÿ
state we do actu. enjoy many sweet
commu. of Pardon of Sin — peace
of Con. — Joy in ÿ ho. G. — increase
of Gr. — & Earnests of Glo. — Rest
from ÿ servitude of Sin, & repose.
our selves in G. till we are prepa.
to rest w him in Glo — Psal. 116. 7.
Return un. ÿ Rest. —
3 an eter. Sab. ÿ remains for ÿ Peo. of G.
— Hea. is a Sab — so ÿ Evening & ÿ
Morn &c — ÿ is to make ÿ ÿ love
Sab. long for hea — & to make
ÿ ÿ long for hea. lo. Sab. —
— ÿ Sab. is a design memo. of Crea.
— of Redemp. — & of Canan a Typ.
Rest of hea — hea. is ÿ Rest —

PAGE OF REV. TIMOTHY JOHNE'S SERMON NOTES.

PRESBYTERIAN PARSONAGE, MORRISTOWN, N. J., OCCUPIED BY REV.
TIMOTHY JOHNES DURING THE REVOLUTION.

Courtesy of Philip H. Hoffman

See page 56

DELL IN THE REAR OF PARSON JOHNE'S RESIDENCE, MORRISTOWN,
N. J., WHERE RELIGIOUS SERVICES WERE HELD
DURING THE REVOLUTION.

Courtesy of Philip H. Hoffm n

See page 248

www.ingramcontent.com/pod-product-compliance
Lightning Source LLC
Chambersburg PA
CBHW071108060525
26252CB00034B/362